inside, outside, upside down

Yasmeen Ismail

Draw &
Discover

Laurence King Publishing

above

Draw some birds flying high above Duck.

below

back

Draw a big picture on the front of Bear's newspaper and some small ones on the back.

front

BEAR NEWS

....-1234..

tall

Rabbit's stack of pancakes is very tall!

Color the pancakes for Rabbit to eat.

Duck's stack
is short.

Add more pancakes
so he has a tall
stack, too.

short

Left

Draw blue birds
on the left side
of the tree.

tweet

right

Draw red birds
on the right
side of the tree.

full

ampoo

empty

Duck's shampoo bottle is empty.
Fill it up again.

What color is
the shampoo?

one

Add lots of bracelets. Decorate them and color them in.

lots

pattern Shhh! Rabbit and Duck are asleep. Color the patterns on their blanket.

plain

Draw some patterns on Bear's plain
blanket, but don't wake him up!

outside

Bear, Rabbit, and Duck are outside a cave.

What can they see inside?

inside

behind

Duck is behind. Rabbit is racing ahead.
Will Duck catch up?

Draw the missing parts of Rabbit's bicycle.

ahead

Bear is holding
his bag right side up.
Color Bear's bag.

right side up

Now Bear's bag is upside down. Draw what's falling out.

upside down

short

Color Bear and his short scarf.

long

Draw a long
scarf around
Bear's neck.

tight

Oof! Bear's hula hoop is squeezing his tummy!

Draw a hula hoop around Duck and Rabbit.
Make it loose, not tight.

Loose

left

Add some yummy food to the shelves on the left.

Now add some more food to the shelves on the right. Yum!

open

Brrr! Rabbit's coat is open.
She is very cold.

Draw Rabbit
with her coat
closed and
buttoned up.

Now she's nice and warm!

closed

short

Bear is big, but his ears are short.
Draw Bear's ears.

long

Rabbit is small, but her ears are long. Draw Rabbit's ears.

Rabbit needs to wear her glasses to read.

off

Put Rabbit's glasses on for her!

on

outside

Rabbit has wrapped a present for Bear.
She's put a big red bow on the outside.

inside

Draw your present for Bear
inside this box.

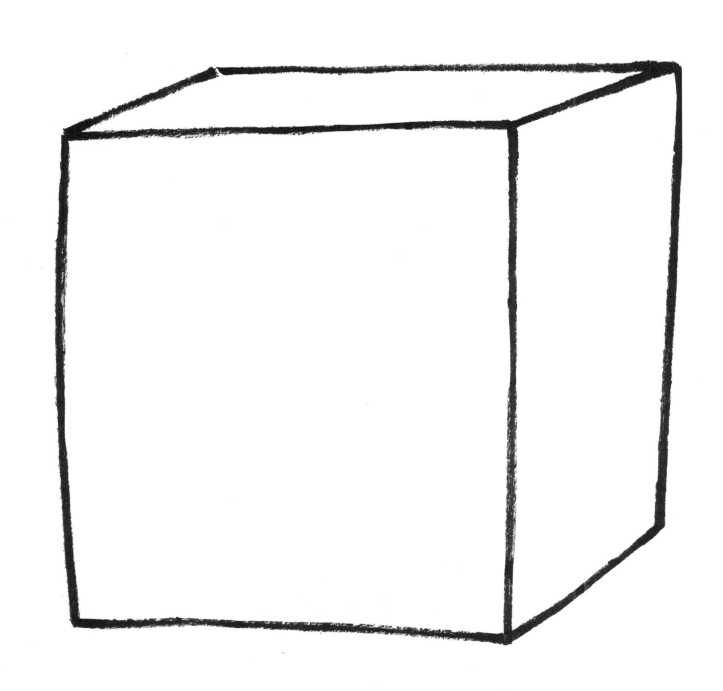

right way up

Duck is the right way up.
Draw a hat on Duck's head.

upside down

Draw Duck upside down!

one

Bear has one balloon.

lots

Draw lots of balloons for Rabbit.

Duck is at the bottom of the ladder.
Rabbit is at the top.

Draw some fruit for Rabbit to pick.

bottom

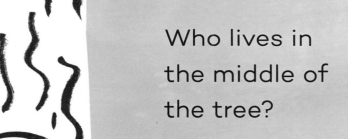

Who lives in
the middle of
the tree?

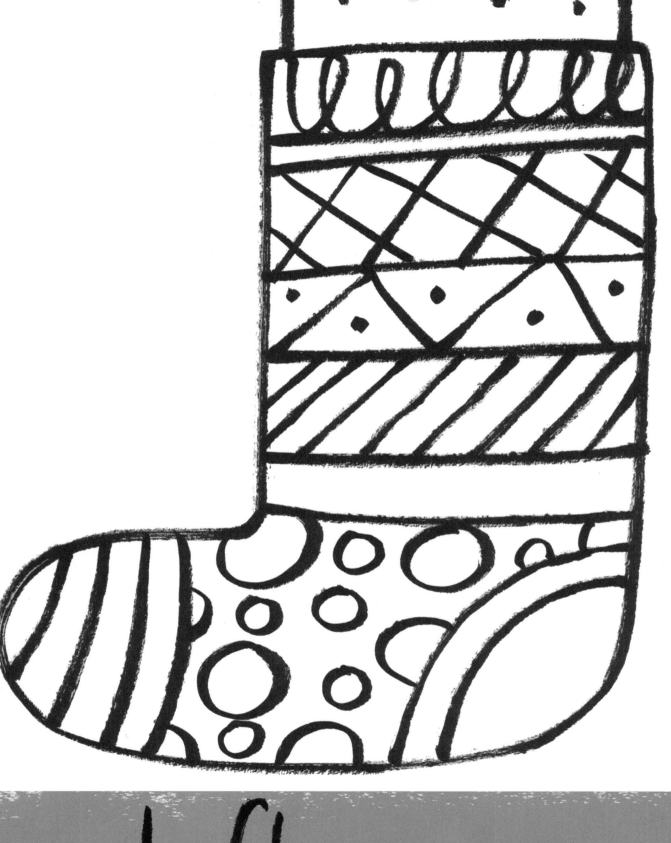

left

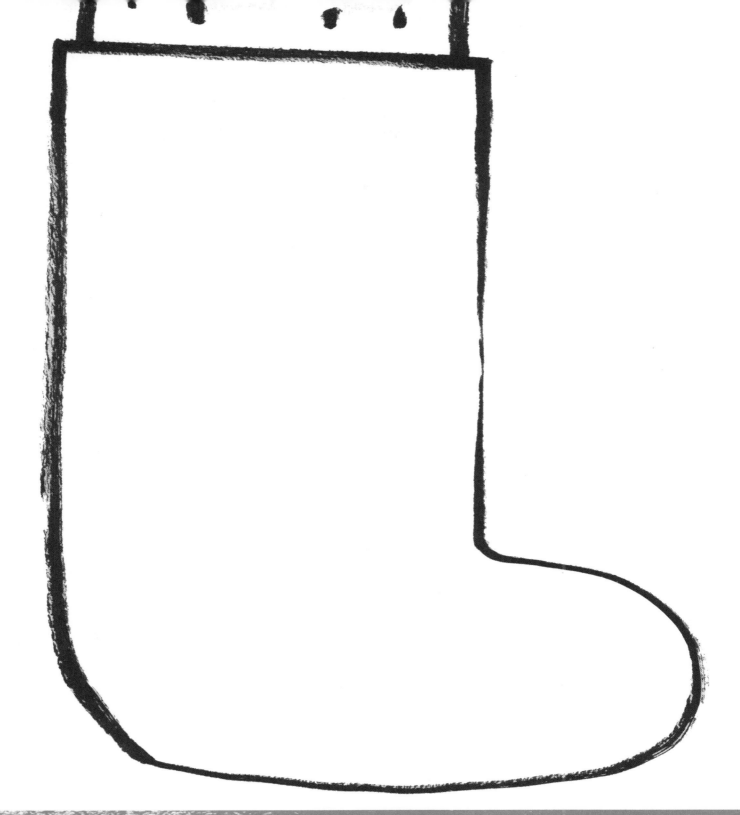

Make the sock on the right match the sock on the left.

right

empty

Duck's cooking pot is empty.
Fill it up with delicious things.
Soon Duck will be full, too!

small

Duck and Bear are on vacation.
Duck has found a very small pyramid.

big

Draw a big pyramid in front of Bear.

long

Oh dear!
Bear's toothbrush is too long.
How will he brush his teeth?

Draw a short
toothbrush so
Bear can brush
his teeth.

short

Duck is swinging very high.

Draw Bear on this low swing.

low

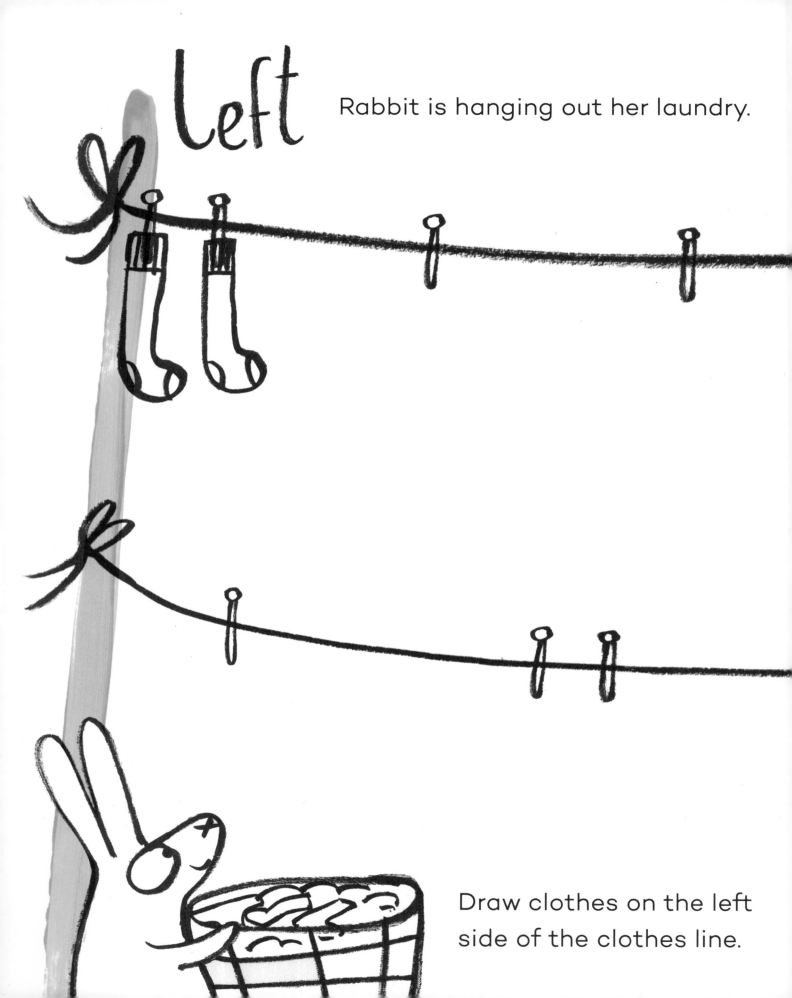

Left

Rabbit is hanging out her laundry.

Draw clothes on the left side of the clothes line.

right

Add more clothes
on the right side.

Blast off!
Draw Duck
and Rabbit
inside the
spaceship.

inside

Duck and Rabbit are exploring outside.

What do they find to put inside their ship to take home?

outside

Draw a picture of yourself upside down!